BARRY SANDERS

FOOTBALL'S RUSHING CHAMP

BY BILL GUTMAN

MILLBROOK SPORTS WORLD

THE MILLBROOK PRESS

BROOKFIELD, CONNECTICUT

Published by The Millbrook Press
2 Old New Milford Road
Brookfield, CT 06804

Created in association with Grey Castle Press, Inc.
Series Editorial Director: *Elizabeth Simon*
Art Director: *Nancy Driscoll*
Design Management: *Italiano-Perla Design*

Photographs courtesy of: John W. McDonough: cover, 3, 7, 44, 46;
AP/Wide World Photos: 4, 10, 16, 20-21, 26, 29, 32, 36, 38-39, 43;
Jerry Clark: 9, 12; Oklahoma State University Athletic Department: 19;
Stillwater Daily News-Press: 22, 24; *Detroit Free Press:* 31.

Library of Congress Cataloging-in-Publication Data

Gutman, Bill.
Barry Sanders, football's rushing champ / by Bill Gutman.
p. cm. — (Millbrook sports world)
Includes bibliographical references (p. 46) and index.
Summary: Describes the life and football career of the college
All-American and Detroit Lions' star running back.
ISBN 1-56294-227-1 (lib. bdg.)
1. Sanders, Barry —Juvenile literature.
2. Football players—United States—
Biography—Juvenile literature.
3. Detroit Lions (Football team) —History—Juvenile literature.
[1. Sanders, Barry 1968- . 2. Football players. 3. Afro-Americans—
Biography] I. Title. II. Series.
GV939.S18G88 1993
796.332'092—dc20
[B]
92-18165 CIP AC

BARRY SANDERS

T he day before Christmas, 1989, was also the final Sunday of the regular National Football League season. The Detroit Lions were visiting the Atlanta Falcons. Neither team was in the running for the playoffs, and only 7,792 fans had paid to witness the game.

But there was some excitement in the air that day. Barry Sanders, the Lions' outstanding rookie running back, had a chance to become the NFL's rushing champion. All he needed was 169 yards and he would surpass Kansas City's fastest, Christian Okoye, whose season was already over.

As had been the case all year, the 5-foot-8 inch (173-centimeter), 203-pound (92-kilogram) Sanders was brilliant. He made darting runs over tackle, changed direction in a flash, and faked out defenders. In the second

In the final game of his rookie season with the Detroit Lions, Barry Sanders ran for 158 yards in a 31-24 victory over the Atlanta Falcons. Here Sanders runs through heavy Falcon traffic en route to a 17-yard touchdown.

period he ran 25 yards for a touchdown. In the third period he broke loose for a 17-yard scoring run. Early in the fourth period he was at it again. This time he ran the ball in from 18 yards out for his third touchdown of the game.

The Atlanta defense was finding out what Chicago Bears' defensive-end Trace Armstrong had learned earlier in the season about Barry Sanders. "I remember bracing myself to hit him," Armstrong said. "I knew I had him. But he just stopped and turned, and he was gone. He's like a little sports car. He can stop on a dime and go zero to 60 in seconds."

Sanders's third touchdown and the extra point gave the Lions a commanding 31-10 lead early in the final period. Then Atlanta began coming back. The Falcons scored a pair of touchdowns to close the gap to 31-24. With one minute left, the Lions got the ball again. All they had to do was run out the clock to win. And there was something else at stake. Detroit coach Wayne Fontes learned that Sanders had run for 158 yards. He needed only 11 more to top Okoye for the overall rushing title.

It seemed a simple matter to send Sanders back into the game and let him run the ball two or three more times. Coach Fontes approached him on the sideline.

"You're 10 yards from catching Okoye," he told the rookie. "Do you want to go back in?"

The answer took the veteran coach by surprise. "Coach," said Sanders, "let's just win it and go home."

Fontes couldn't believe it. He asked Sanders whether or not there was a bonus clause in his contract that would give him more money for winning the rushing title. But Sanders declined to reenter the game and said simply:

Several times during his career, Barry Sanders has remained on the sidelines to let others play even though he could have easily added to his own statistics and won even more awards.

"Coach, give the ball to Tony [fullback Tony Paige]. Let's just win it and go home."

And that's what happened. The Lions ran out the clock and won the game. Barry Sanders finished his first pro season with 1,470 yards, 10 fewer than rushing champion Okoye. It didn't matter to him; Sanders never worried about records or his numbers.

"When everyone is out for statistics or individual fulfillment, that's when trouble starts," he said. "I don't ever want to fall victim to that."

Asked later if he regretted not winning the rushing title when it was so close, Sanders just shook his head. "I satisfied my ego last season," he said.

Barry Sanders was an unusual athlete. He was not in sports for personal glory. And yet he broke perhaps more records than any running back before him. He never aimed for awards. But he received some of the biggest awards a football player could earn. He was now called the best running back in pro football, following in the footsteps of such runners as Jim Brown, Gale Sayers, O. J. Simpson, Tony Dorsett, and Walter Payton.

When Payton, who retired as the NFL's all-time leading rusher, saw Barry Sanders play as a rookie, he said flat out, "I don't know if I was ever that good!"

YOUTH AT RISK

Although Barry Sanders was one of the great runners in pro football, he didn't act like a star athlete. He didn't go in for fancy clothes or jewelry. He didn't brag about his talent. He didn't smoke, drink, or swear.

Nowadays, Barry Sanders might seem too good to be true, but things were different earlier in his life. When Barry was born on July 16, 1968, in Wichita, Kansas, he became the seventh of William and Shirley Sanders's eleven children. Eventually, there were eight girls and three boys growing up under the same roof. William Sanders was a carpenter and roofer and didn't always have steady work, so the family never had much money.

Barry and his brothers had a wild streak. The oldest, Boyd, became involved with drugs at one point but straightened himself out. Boyd went on to become a minister and was a positive influence on Barry's life.

Barry was closest to his brother Byron, who was about a year older. The two boys shared a room at home and before long were sharing trouble.

"I got into fights and did a lot of wrong," said Barry, looking back on his pre-teen days. "Byron and I stole candy and were always having fights at school."

That wasn't all. The two brothers often threw rocks at passing cars, and Barry once started a fire in the bathroom of their house. Another time, the two brothers were arrested for trespassing at near-by Wichita State University. They would sometimes sneak into the stadium and play a game where they would hop up and down the stadium steps.

Some of it was just young boys having fun, but some was dangerous. Barry admits that now. "It's a fine line between going right and wrong," he said. "Sometimes I wonder why I've been so fortunate."

There were two reasons why young Barry turned out all right. One was his parents, and the other was sports. William Sanders was a strict parent who tried to keep his kids in line. He was always direct about what he expected from his children and never hid his feelings.

Young Barry was always small for his age.

"My dad always shot straight," Barry said."He didn't beat around the bush."

Mr. and Mrs. Sanders were also very religious people. Although it took a while for what they said to make an impression, their values were important

Shirley and William Sanders were always proud of their son, but never more than when Barry won the 1988 Heisman Trophy as the best college football player in the land.

to their family. The children were taught to have humility, as well as a firm belief in themselves.

The children brought these values to sports as well. Barry and Byron began playing early. Barry's first love was basketball. In fact, he said that game is still his favorite sport. He also played football as a kid, and it was apparent from the beginning that it was his best sport.

The boys played wild games, sometimes with twenty players on a side. That's how Barry says he learned how to avoid tacklers so well. There were times in those games when ten would-be tacklers were coming after him at once. He had to try hard to avoid them. Otherwise, he would have gotten beaten up.

Barry became one of the stars of the neighborhood pickup games. But he grew slowly. His size worked against him for a long time. He was small when he went to Bryant Elementary School and still small at Hadley Junior High. There was no football at either school, so at that time he had to play in the Greater Wichita Youth Football League. He started in the sixth grade and stayed with it right into the ninth grade. All he ever heard about was his size.

"I never knew how good I could be then because everyone was always telling me I was too small," he said. "Everyone but my father. He told me I could be great. I know people think that was just a father talking, but he always told me the truth." Barry was determined to prove his father right.

A HIGH SCHOOL POWER

When Barry entered North High School in Wichita in the fall of 1983, he assumed that the only way he might be able to play football would be as defensive back. Only William Sanders saw his son as a running back. Everyone else had their doubts because of his size. Those big tacklers, ends, and linebackers would crush him.

Barry played both football and basketball in high school. He loved to run with the football. Yet the coaches still didn't play him very much. During

those games William Sanders would sometimes sit in the stands and yell at the coaches: "Play him! Let him run!"

During Barry's sophomore year he played on the junior varsity team, although he did see some varsity action as a safety.

"Barry always had great speed," said Dennis Brunner, who was the defensive backfield coach when Barry was at North High. "His job was to defend against deep passes. He was so fast that if someone broke away, Barry could run him down."

Dennis Brunner also said that Barry worked hard in both the classroom and on the football field. He was about 5 feet 5 (165 centimeters) when he arrived at North High and weighed about 140 pounds (64 kilograms). He gradually got bigger and stronger. Although he would never be tall, he was on his way to becoming a solid 175 pounds (79 kilograms) before he graduated.

When Barry was a junior, head coach Bob Shepler talked about making him a tailback and giving him a chance to carry the ball. But Barry wouldn't do it. The reason was simple: His brother Byron was the starting tailback, and Barry didn't want to compete with him.

Barry started as defensive back and played wingback on offense. The team used a slot-I formation in which the running backs are right behind the quarterback. Barry played wingback and lined up to the side of the quarter-

It was still hard to envision Barry as a future All-American in this picture, taken before the start of his senior year at North High School in Wichita.

back. The wingback rarely carried the football. He was more of a pass receiver, and Dennis Brunner said Barry was a good one.

"We were all very pleased with Byron Sanders at tailback," Brunner remembers. "Byron was a good football player, a little bigger than Barry, but not as fast. Yet I never forgot something that William Sanders said to me during a scrimmage when Barry was a sophomore. He came up to me and said that the sophomore was going to be the football player. I was pleased with Byron, but the father must have sensed something special in Barry."

By the time he was a senior, Barry was close to 170 pounds (77 kilograms). He was also becoming a fine runner. Byron Sanders was off to college, and Dale Burkholder was the new head coach at North High School. In the third game of the season Barry was moved from wingback to tailback. He took off.

"I can still see him out there doing things that seem impossible," Dennis Brunner recalls. "As fast as he was, he could stop on a dime and reverse his field before the defense could even react. He made some dazzling runs and was fabulous all year."

It wasn't long before Barry was putting together a string of great games. The best came against Emporia High when he ran for more than 300 yards. Finally, in the last game against East High Barry did something very unusual for someone so young. His team was winning the game easily, and Barry was taken out to give some other players an opportunity to play. Then someone noticed that Barry needed only another 30 yards to become the league's leading rusher.

But Barry refused go back in. As he would do later on in pro football, he told the coach the game was won. The rushing title wasn't important, he said. This was the first time he let others get their chance to play instead of seeking personal glory.

That kind of humility would become a Sanders trademark. Individual glory was not for him. As it turned out, he gained more than 1,500 yards as a senior at North High. He was named to both the All-City and All-State teams.

"Barry was a quiet kid, never bragged about himself, or did anything to draw attention to himself," Dennis Brunner said. "He was very religious even then and popular with the other students. In fact, I had six members of his family in my classes over the years and they were all fine kids."

Despite Barry's brilliant senior year on the gridiron, the colleges did not rush to recruit him. In fact, for a while it seemed that no one wanted him.

Coach Burkholder put together a highlight film, showing a series of Barry's great runs. Some colleges, like Nebraska, returned it without even watching it.

"His size was the big thing," Dennis Brunner said. "He wasn't tall, and a lot of the recruiters didn't feel he could hold much more weight on his compact body."

William Sanders always wanted his son to play for the University of Oklahoma, but the Sooners never even followed up after writing Barry a recruiting letter. Even local schools had little or no interest in Barry. Wichita State (just two blocks from the Sanders home), the University of Kansas, and Kansas State all declined to offer him a scholarship.

"It's amazing to me how much attention coaches and scouts pay to size," Barry said, looking back. "I think that's where a lot of them fail. The fact that most of the big schools ignored me gave me incentive to show them that it's not all about size."

He finally got offers from Tulsa and Iowa State. Then Oklahoma State University entered the picture. It seems that the people at OSU saw the same

Not too many colleges wanted to give Barry a football scholarship when he graduated from high school. Luckily Coach Pat Jones of Oklahoma State did. Here coach and star runner sit together at a press conference.

highlight film that Nebraska refused to look at. Assistant coach George Walstad saw it, and was so impressed by Barry's running that he talked head coach Pat Jones into offering Barry a scholarship.

The fall after Barry's graduation from North High School he was headed to Stillwater, Oklahoma, to start his freshman year. It would take another three years before Barry Sanders would show the football world what he had.

IN THE WINGS

When Barry arrived at Stillwater he was nearly 5 feet 8 (173 centimeters) and weighed 180 pounds (82 kilograms). All the time he was at Oklahoma State he lifted weights to increase his strength. When he joined the football squad as a freshman, he got both good news and bad news. The good news was that the Cowboys used the I-formation that Barry had played in high school. He could play tailback once again. The bad news was that the team already had an outstanding tailback in junior Thurman Thomas.

Thomas wasn't much bigger than Barry. He was 5 feet 10 (178 centimeters), about 190 pounds (86 kilograms), and a quick and elusive runner. As a sophomore in 1985 he had run for 1,650 yards on 327 carries and was named to several All-American teams. Thomas was a star, and there was no way that Barry, as a freshman, could hope to replace him.

Perhaps it was good that Barry wasn't pressured to perform right away. It gave him a chance to grow and mature. He was spotted in a few games, enough to give him a taste of big-time college football. But Thomas remained number one.

Barry carried the ball just 74 times as a freshman, gaining 325 yards and scoring a pair of touchdowns. When he came back for his sophomore season in 1987, he knew he would again be second string. Thomas still saw the bulk of the action.

Barry became the Cowboys' top kickoff and punt return man. His quickness amazed people. He could stop, change direction, and cut while defenders stalled and stumbled. He was exciting to watch.

So while Thurman Thomas ran his way to yet another All-American season in 1987, Barry Sanders was also quietly making a name for himself. He saw enough action to carry the ball 111 times, gaining 622 yards for an impressive 5.6 average. In three games he went over the 100-yard mark. Better yet, he showed he had a nose for the goal line, scoring nine touchdowns. He caught four passes for 58 yards and another touchdown.

He did all this in a backup role to Thomas. It was as a kickoff and punt returner that Barry made a name for himself in 1987. He led the nation with a 3.13 average for 15 kickoff returns, bringing back two for touchdowns, one a dazzling run of 100 yards. He was second in the nation with a 15.2 average on 18 punt returns. On two of those returns he wound up in the end zone, including one twisting, turning run of 73 yards.

Barry came from nowhere to become the most electrifying kick returner in all of college football. For his efforts, *The Sporting News* named him to their All-American team as the kick return specialist.

As for Thurman Thomas, he wound up his OSU career with more than 1,600 yards rushing and was once again an All-American choice. He was the second-round draft choice of the Buffalo Bills and became a star in the NFL.

Barry Sanders had spent two years waiting in the wings. Now he looked forward to the 1988 season. He would get a chance to do what his father had always wanted him to do—run with the football.

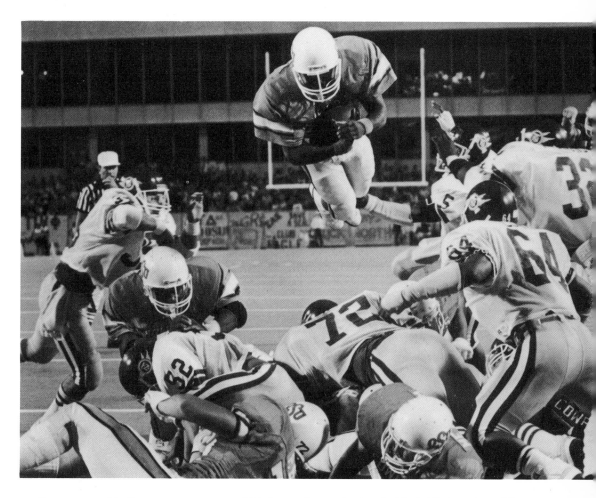

Barry spent his first two seasons at Oklahoma State playing behind All-American Thurman Thomas (flying through the air with the ball). When Thomas left, Barry became an All-American and later both runners were National Football League All-Pros.

RECORD-BREAKING YEAR

Barry returned for his junior year bigger and stronger than ever. He was still 5 feet 8 (173 centimeters), but now packed nearly 200 pounds (91 kilograms) on his sturdy frame. His work with weights had paid off. It had made him stronger, yet he had lost none of his speed and quickness. Strangely enough, in the early practice sessions, Coach Jones said that Barry would still have to win a job.

"We knew we had something very good in Barry last year. He played that well," said Coach Jones. "But you couldn't predict what he was going to do this year. Going into the season, he wasn't as experienced as Thomas had been, and he hadn't proven a lot of things."

It didn't take Barry long to prove himself. He was surrounded by a number of fine offensive players, including quarter-

Many defenders who tried to tackle Barry in the open field ended up grabbing at air, like the Texas A & M player shown here.

back Mike Gundy and wide receiver Hart Lee Dykes. The club had a fine blocking fullback and a senior offensive line. As the season unfolded, the offensive line dedicated itself to blocking for Barry. The Cowboys' defense had a lot of holes in it. So the offense knew from the beginning that they would have to score big to win.

The team opened the year with a couple of big victories, topping Miami of Ohio, 52-20, and Texas A & M, 52-15. The offense was working. Barry

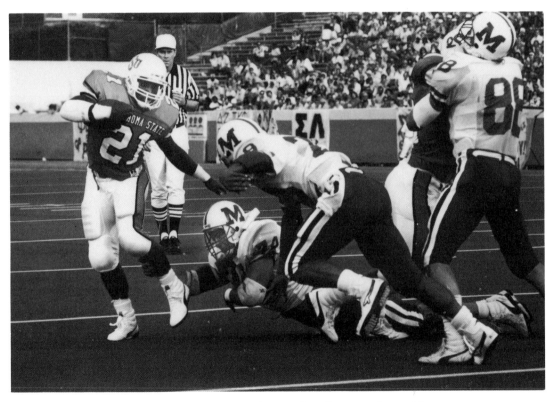

Once he became a starter as a junior, Barry's speed and power showed in every game. Against Miami of Ohio in the opener he ran for 178 yards as Oklahoma State won, 52-20.

also had a good start. He gained 178 yards in the opener and 157 more in the game against A & M. He also scored two touchdowns in each game. But it was in the third game against Tulsa that the nation began to learn about the rushing ability of Barry Sanders.

Barry was all over the field. He slashed between the tackles and sprinted around the ends. He darted through the smallest hole and changed direction so quickly that he was often hard to follow. He carried the ball 33 times that day and set a new OSU record by gaining 304 yards. He also scored five big touchdowns as the Cowboys won again, 56-35. Now Coach Jones was convinced of Barry's ability.

"He's the most explosive guy I've ever seen. He sees an opening, and he can be at full-speed, bam, just like that. Plus he's so strong and tough that people just can't tackle him."

Quarterback Gundy had a bird's eye view of Barry's talent. He would hand his tailback the ball, then watch him go to work.

"By the time the defensive guys see him, he's usually by them," said Gundy. "Then what he does five or six yards down the field is even better. Guys will come up and take a stab at him, and he'll make one quick move and never slow down. They don't even touch him. It's the most amazing thing I've ever seen."

As the season wore on, Barry not only kept up the pace, he got better and better. After 174 yards in a 41-21 win over Colorado, he got 189 yards on 35 carries against powerful Nebraska. The OSU defense faltered in this one, and the Cornhuskers won, 63-42. But Barry had scored four touchdowns against both Colorado and Nebraska, two outstanding teams.

*Barry shows his heels to a trio of Tulsa defenders as he sets an Oklahoma State
record by running for 304 yards on 33 carries. He also scored 5 touchdowns as
the Cowboys won, 56-35.*

After he cruised to a 154-yard game in an easy 49-21 win over Missouri,
he exploded again. This time he made headlines by running for 320 yards on
37 carries in a 45-27 win over Kansas State. He ate up the Kansas State
defense all afternoon, crossing the goal line three times.

Although Barry was just 5 feet 8 (173 centimeters), he was by no means
small. He was extremely strong for his size: He had wide shoulders and

huge thighs that measured 37 inches (94 centimeters) around, as big as many linemen's. They gave him power and durability. "We were worried about overworking him," said Pat Jones. "But he never got hurt and never seemed tired. On Mondays we told him he could back off a bit, but he always refused and took a full workload."

His great season continued. He had 215 yards in a 31-28 loss to arch-rival Oklahoma. Then he exploded again, gaining 312 yards on 37 carries, scoring another five touchdowns as OSU topped Kansas, 63-24. He was the leading rusher in the country and seemed on the way to a record-breaking season.

Barry was getting more unstoppable each week. He had 293 yards and four more touchdowns in a 49-28 win over Iowa State. He was also close to breaking Marcus Allen's single-season NCAA rushing mark, set in 1981. The last game of the 1988 season, against Texas Tech, was held in Japan. It was a special game called the Coca-Cola Classic. While the teams were in Japan, the winner of the Heisman Trophy would be announced. The trophy is given to the best college football player in the United States. Reporters followed Barry everywhere in Japan.

"It's [the Heisman Trophy] just not that big a deal for me," he said. "And it's not really fair to so many other people. People take sports so seriously. To some of them, sports is a god, which is wrong."

For Barry, there was another message that was more important to him. "I know I have an opportunity to be a positive influence on young people," he said. "I have never used drugs. I try to study and stay out of trouble."

Shortly before the game against Texas Tech, Barry learned he had won the Heisman Trophy, topping quarterbacks Rodney Peete of USC and Troy

Aikman of UCLA in the voting. Then he went out and ran for a career-best 332 yards on 44 carries as OSU blasted Texas Tech, 45-42.

If Barry wasn't overjoyed at winning the Heisman, his linemen were. Some of them wept. "We're so proud and happy for him," said guard Chris Stanley. "He's a great guy, and we all knew how hard he worked for it. When I sat next to him on the plane coming home from Tokyo, he didn't act any differently."

His teammates had nothing but respect for the tailback they called "Rocket Man." As quarterback Gundy said, "If I had a kid, I'd want him to grow up to be like Barry. Not because of his great athletic ability, but because of the kind of person he is."

Barry Sanders put together a miraculous season, breaking and setting 21 NCAA records. He wound up with 2,628 yards and 344 carries for an amazing 7.6 average. He topped Allen's record of 2,342 yards with 59 fewer carries. He also set a new mark by averaging 238.9 yards per game. He scored the most rushing touchdowns in a season (37), the most points (234), and had four, 300-yard games. No other player had more than one 300-yard game in an entire career.

He also set a new record with 3,250 all-purpose yards, and a record for all-purpose yards per game with an average of 295.5. Barry Sanders had been amazing. Needless to say, he was a consensus All-American and won

A very proud Barry Sanders poses with the Heisman Trophy, the biggest award a college football player can win.

a number of other 1988 Player-of-the-Year awards. His coach, Pat Jones, said, "I don't think there's any question he's the finest player in college football today."

TO THE NFL

There was still one more game to play. In December 1989, the Cowboys faced Wyoming in the Holiday Bowl, and once again Barry was the center of attention. He ran for 222 yards as OSU crushed their opponents, 62-14. Late in the game, Barry needed just three more yards to break the Bowl rushing record, and as usual he declined to go back in.

"They told me I was three yards away, but it didn't mean anything to me at all," he said. "Coach Jones asked me if I wanted some more. I told him I'd rather not."

Even his coach knew that Barry was not in the game for individual glory. If he were, his record would have been even more amazing.

"If we had left him in some games, he could have had another 1,000 yards easy," said the coach.

Barry still had one more year remaining at Oklahoma State. But he also had the option of applying for the NFL draft. At first all signs were that he would return for his senior year. He was a physical education major and always had good grades.

But several people, including his father, pointed out that it would be hard for him to top what he had done in 1988. If Barry's numbers were down, people might think something wasn't right. There was always the risk of

This is a typical scene Oklahoma State fans would never forget: Barry Sanders bursting past defenders for big yardage. Soon after, he announced he would pass up his senior year to become a professional in the NFL.

injury. If he blew out a knee, his value would go down. But the overriding factor was his family's financial situation. They just didn't have a lot of money. Finally, Barry made the announcement everyone had been waiting for: He would not return to OSU for his senior year.

"I've come to the conclusion that it would be in my best interests and my family's best interests to renounce my last year of eligibility and pursue a career in professional football."

The stage was set. The NFL approved Barry's application, and he was made part of the draft on April 23, 1989. Right away there was a guessing game as to which team would pick him. Most of the scouts put him at the top of the list of running backs coming out. Dallas had the first pick in the draft and took quarterback Troy Aikman. Green Bay was next, and they picked Michigan State offensive tackle Tony Mandarich. Next came the Detroit Lions. The Lions had been looking for defensive help, but when Barry became available, their plans changed. A group of coaches went to Stillwater to watch him work out. That did it. The Lions made him their first-round pick, the third player taken in the draft. Sanders was headed to Detroit.

At first, Sanders and the Lions couldn't agree on a contract. He became a holdout during the pre-season and didn't sign a contract until three days before the regular season began. It was a five-year, $6.1 million pact. Some fans and members of the media felt he was only another greedy athlete. But Sanders didn't want the money just for himself. He helped his entire family, then did something not many athletes have done. He immediately sent a check for $210,000 to the Baptist church in Wichita that he had attended while growing up. His charitable work hasn't stopped since.

Although he had missed the entire pre-season and all the exhibition games, Barry was finally part of the team. He was ready to go.

A SPECIAL KIND OF ROOKIE

It had been a rough few years for the Detroit Lions. They were a proud, old NFL franchise and were coming off five straight losing seasons. The team was rebuilding, with its future in the hands of players like Barry Sanders.

The Lions also drafted quarterback Rodney Peete of USC, one of Sanders's rivals for the Heisman. But Peete was starting the season on the injured list.

Because Sanders had missed all of the pre-season, he hadn't practiced the plays. The Lions opened up against the Phoenix Cardinals. Phoenix had a 6-3 lead with 5:34 left in the third quarter when the rookie Sanders got into the game for the first time.

He carried four straight times for 29 yards, finishing the drive with a 3-yard touchdown run. With no real practice, Sanders was already showing his stuff. The Cards would go on to win the game, 16-13, but Sanders stayed in to carry the ball nine times for 71 yards, an average of almost 8 yards each time.

It's a new beginning for Sanders as he plays his first game for the Detroit Lions in September 1989. Sanders was a little rusty, and Phoenix Cardinals tacklers often stopped him for short gains.

"He only knew four plays, two left and two right," said Coach Fontes. "He ran the same play over and over and over again, and they all looked different. That's the sign of a great back."

Sanders still needed to get in game shape. He had just 57 yards on 12 carries in a loss to the Giants the next week. The following week it began to come together. Although the Lions lost to the powerful Chicago Bears, 47-27, rookie Sanders was once again a force. He ran for 126 yards on 18 car-

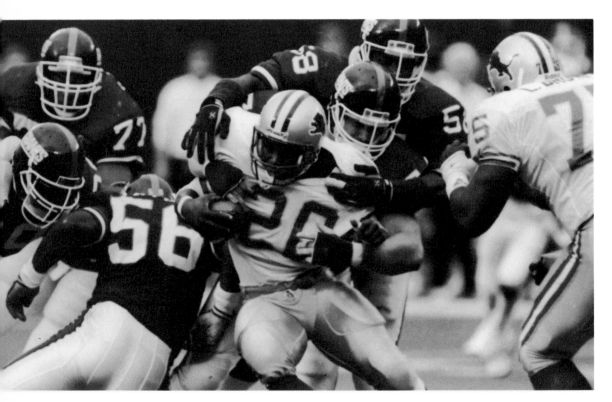

In a loss to the New York Giants during his rookie year, Sanders found the defense tough to crack. Wherever he went, three, four, or five Giants tacklers were there to meet him.

ries, outgaining the Bears All-Pro, Neal Anderson. After three games he had 254 yards and a 6.5 per carry average. That wasn't bad for a guy who didn't have any practice before the season began. But the Bears game had taken a toll. Sanders suffered from a bruised hip and carried the ball just five times for one yard the next week in a loss to the Steelers.

"It won't happen again," he said. "Before the first game I was going to wear my hip pads, but when I learned that a number of guys didn't wear them, I didn't either. But I definitely learned why the Lord invented hip pads."

The hip was a problem. He gained 99 yards against Minnesota, then had to sit out as the team won its first game against Tampa Bay. Finally, in week eight, Sanders exploded. It came against divisional rival Green Bay. The Packers would win the game in overtime, 23-20, but not until Barry Sanders burned them for 184 yards on 30 carries. He was all over the field, darting through holes, breaking tackles, and faking defenders.

"He runs so low to the ground and is so strong and elusive that it makes it very difficult to get a piece of him," said Green Bay linebacker Brian Noble. "You never get the shot at him. Usually, when you get to him, he's not there anymore."

Minnesota Viking tacklers had such a hard time stopping him that they accused him of spraying himself with silicone before the game to make himself slippery. The referees actually checked him, but there was no slippery substance on his uniform. It was just his way of running.

After nine weeks, the Lions were in last place with a 1-8 record. Sanders, however, was the fourth best rusher in the National Football Conference

(NFC) with 688 yards on 131 carries for a 5.3 average. He had been good, with flashes of greatness.

He had a solid, 114-yard day against Cincinnati in the 11th game, but the Lions lost again, 42-7. A week later Sanders was a big factor as the Lions topped the Cleveland Browns, 13-10. In that one the rookie gained 145 yards on 28 carries. After 12 games he had moved into the NFC rushing lead with 1,016 yards on 193 tries.

Rookie Sanders was making believers out of a lot of people. Both he and the Lions were finishing strong. Sanders gained 120 yards and scored twice in a 27-17 victory over the Bears. He then had 104 in a 33-7 triumph over the Bucs, and finished with that 158-yard effort against the Falcons as the Lions won, 31-24. That was the game in which Sanders decided not to go back in despite having a chance to win the overall NFL rushing title.

Detroit had won six of their last seven games, including five in a row, giving the team an overall 7-9 record. Sanders led the NFC with 1,470 yards on 280 carries for a 5.3 average and he scored 14 touchdowns. He had earned the respect of everyone.

"When you defend against Barry you have to start by finding him," said Bears All-Pro linebacker Mike Singletary. "Then you have to tackle him with good technique. If you try to blast him, chances are he'll spin out of it, and you'll end up looking a little silly."

Oddly enough, Sanders's longest run of the season was only 34 yards. The fact that he didn't have any 75- or 80-yard runs showed how consistent he was. The team was also using a new, pass-oriented, run-and-shoot offense called "The Silver Stretch." It started to work toward the end of the year. Offensive coordinator Mouse Davis said the best was yet to come.

"Wait till the Stretch starts clicking," he said. "Teams will have to use six defensive backs against it. Barry will flat tear that up. In fact, if we'd have been first or second, or even 10th in passing instead of 26th, Barry would have broken the rushing record."

ALL-PRO AND GETTING BETTER

Sanders proved himself an exciting and durable runner as a first-year pro. He was chosen 1989 NFL Rookie of the Year. He was also named to play in the Pro Bowl and was a member of several All-Pro teams. You couldn't do much more as a rookie. There was talk of his someday breaking Eric Dickerson's single season rushing mark of 2,105 yards. But, as usual, Sanders didn't even want to talk about individual records.

"Oh, I don't know," he answered when asked about his chances to break the mark. "Nothing ever turns out the way people expect it to."

The Lions didn't look good in their first 1990 game. They lost to Tampa Bay, 38-21. It was a big disappointment since the team had finished the 1989 season with five straight wins. The club won the next week, beating Atlanta, 21-14. But Sanders had only 55 yards on 18 carries and had gained 134 yards in the first two games. Opposing defenses were stacking up to stop him. Unless the Lions developed a consistent passing game, Sanders would find the going tough.

By the end of his rookie year, Barry Sanders was again the great all-around runner he had been at Oklahoma State. Here, tacklers sprawl on the ground as he bursts past them.

"Nobody's pass-rushing," said Coach Fontes. "Teams have had six guys watching Barry Sanders, just waiting for him. When they see he doesn't have the ball, then they start rushing."

Sanders, of course, never complained. He just kept trying his best. The team was again having injury problems on the defense, and the passing game wasn't good. Because Sanders wasn't a great pass blocker, Coach Fontes sometimes pulled him out of the lineup in passing situations.

After six weeks the team was 2-4. Sanders was among the league leaders in rushing, but Coach Fontes was complaining about Sanders's ability as a pass receiver: "He just has trouble eluding people when he doesn't have the ball."

In fairness, Sanders had never been used much as a receiver, neither in college nor as an NFL rookie. His former OSU teammate, Thurman Thomas, had developed into an outstanding receiver as well as a fine runner. Sanders was a great runner. Now he had to work on his all-around game.

Part of the problem was that the Lions couldn't settle on a quarterback. Rodney Peete was the starter, but missed a lot of games due to injuries. His replacement, Bob Gagliano, wasn't considered a top passer. That made it tough for Sanders to develop as a receiver.

It was the defense that got credit for a 27-10 win over New Orleans. But an overtime loss to Washington, 41-38, left the team at 3-5 at the halfway mark. Surprisingly, Barry was not among the top five rushers in the league. The problem was with the entire offense. It was still inconsistent. Many felt that if the Lions were going to win, their prize runner would have to get the ball more often. In the fourth quarter and the overtime against Washington, he carried the ball just twice.

It was a strange year. The Lions finished at 6-10. Most of the talk was about the quarterback question and the passing game. When healthy, Rodney Peete looked as if he could do the job. Sanders was almost in the

background. Yet when the season ended, he was the NFL's rushing champion with 1,304 yards on 255 carries. His three biggest games came in the 11th, 13th, and 15th weeks. In those games he had 147, 176, and 133 yards. He also caught 35 passes on the season for another 462 yards. For a player who wasn't supposed to catch, that was quite a record. But in the closing weeks he had become the focal point of the offense again. As a result, he was a Pro Bowler and All-Pro choice a second time.

One analysis of the team put it this way. "Although they use the run-and-shoot, the Lions have learned that their success is linked to running-back Barry Sanders. The offense will continue to conjure ways of getting the ball to Sanders."

Sanders finished his second pro season as the NFL rushing champion with 1,304 yards. This was the Lions' final game against Seattle, in which Sanders clinched the title.

That seemed to be the case in 1991. The team made some changes to get the ball to Sanders more often. Quarterback Peete was playing well. Bruised ribs kept Sanders out of the first game, and the powerful Washington Redskins buried the Lions, 45-0. The long-suffering Detroit fans figured it was more of the same.

A week later, things began to change. Detroit beat arch-rival Green Bay, 23-14, with Sanders returning to run for 42 yards. He still wasn't 100 percent. But against Miami in week three he was. This time he ran for 143 yards on 32 tries as the Lions won again, 17-13. A 33-24 win over the Colts followed with Sanders running wild for 179 yards on 30 carries. The Lions were getting him the ball now, and the team was a surprising 3-1.

The numbers continued to be impressive. Sanders got 160 yards in a 31-3 win over Tampa Bay, followed by a 116-yard day as Detroit toppled Minnesota, 24-20. It was truly a team effort that brought the Lions to a 5-1 mark.

A big 35-3 loss to the 49ers brought the team back to earth. The San Francisco defense was geared to stop Sanders, and they did. Barry had just seven carries for 26 yards. He got only 55 yards against Dallas, but caught a key 10-yard scoring pass from backup quarterback Erik Kramer to help salt away a 34-10 victory.

A mid-season slump left the team at 6-4, but after 10 games Sanders was leading the NFC in rushing with 902 yards. Interestingly, college teammate Thurman Thomas of Buffalo led the AFC with 968 yards. The former Oklahoma State players were now perhaps the two best running backs in the NFL. Sanders was considered the better pure runner, and Thomas the better pass receiver out of the backfield. At that point in the

season the Lions turned it on. Kramer was at quarterback for the injured
Peete. The defense was much better, and the team was virtually unbeatable
at home in the Pontiac Silverdome. They didn't lose again for the rest of the
regular season. They won their final six straight games.

Against the Vikings in week 12, Barry Sanders had his greatest game as a
pro. He rushed 23 times for 220 yards, scoring on touchdown runs of 17,
45, 4, and 9 yards. In addition, he caught four passes for 31 yards as Detroit
won, 34-14.

"It was one of those days I've been waiting for all year long," he said
afterward. From there the Lions coasted home. They won the NFC Central
Division title with a 12-4 record—the surprise team of the year. Better yet,
they were in the playoffs.

Barry Sanders also had his greatest year as a pro. He rushed for 1,548
yards on 342 carries, an average of 4.5 a try. He led the league with 17
touchdowns, 16 coming on the ground. It was his third All-Pro year. He
caught 41 passes for another 307 yards.

Yet through it all, he still rarely talked about himself or his talents. "There
isn't a braggart's breath in Barry Sanders's body," wrote one reporter.

The important thing now was the playoffs. In their first playoff game
against Dallas, the Lions looked great. With the Dallas defense set to stop
Sanders, Erik Kramer and his teammates came out throwing. They marched
through the air to an easy 38-6 victory. Sanders carried just 12 times, but
gained 69 yards and scored a touchdown.

Now it was on to the NFC title game against Washington, the team that
had crushed them in the opener. The winner would be going to the Super
Bowl. It was a close game early. In the first quarter, Sanders looked almost

unstoppable. He had 46 yards on just six carries. That's when the Redskins made an adjustment.

For the rest of the game, the Skins' defense keyed on Sanders. Quarterback Kramer wasn't having a good day, and the strategy worked. Detroit trailed just 10-7 midway through the second quarter. It was 17-10 at halftime. In the second half Washington ran away. The Redskins won 41-10. Sanders wound up with 44 yards on 11 carries.

It had still been one of the Lions' most successful seasons in years. With an offense built around Barry Sanders, the team became a big winner in 1991, and they hoped to continue to win.

Since becoming a starter as a junior at Oklahoma State in 1988, Barry Sanders has never had a bad year. In fact, so far he has had only great years. He has not had a serious injury. Even with more than 300 carries a year, he has run hard every time. Those who used to say he was too small must have eaten their words. He has been as tough as they come.

Success hasn't spoiled Barry Sanders. He has remained close to his family and attends Bible and prayer meetings regularly. Perhaps it was his coach with the Lions, Wayne Fontes, who summed up his star runner the best.

"Barry doesn't wear his beliefs on his sleeve," Fontes said. "He's not the type of guy who scores a touchdown and kneels down in front of everyone in the world. He's not for show; he's for real."

In the 1991 playoffs, the Lions made it all the way to the NFC championship game, where they were beaten by the Washington Redskins. Here Sanders looks for running room against the tough Washington defense, as cornerback Alvoid Mays moves in to stop him.

BARRY SANDERS: HIGHLIGHTS

1968   Born on July 16 in Wichita, Kansas.

1983   Plays defensive back and wingback for North High School in Wichita.

1985   Plays tailback in his senior year at North High School.
                Named to the All-City (Wichita) and All-State (Kansas) teams.

1986   Earns a scholarship to Oklahoma State University.

1987   Named to *The Sporting News*'s All-American team as the kick-return specialist.

1988   Receives Heisman Trophy.
                Sets 21 NCAA records.
                Named consensus All-American and receives numerous Player-of-the-Year
                    awards.

1989   Picked by the Detroit Lions in the first round of the NFL draft.
                Leads NFC with 1,470 yards on 280 carries for a 5.3 average.
                Named NFL Rookie of the Year.
                Named to play in Pro Bowl and also named to several All-Pro teams.

1990   Becomes NFL rushing champion with 1,304 yards on 255 carries.
                Named to Pro Bowl and All-Pro teams.

1991   Helps lead the Lions to win the NFC Central Division title.
                Rushes for 1,548 yards on 342 carries, and leads the league with 17 touchdowns.
                Named to All-Pro team.

FIND OUT MORE

Anderson, Dave. *The Story of Football*. New York: Morrow Junior Books, 1985.

Duden, Jane and Susan Osberg. *Football*. New York: Macmillan, 1991.

National Football League. *Good Days, Bad Days*. New York: Viking, 1992.

Rothaus, James R. *Detroit Lions*. Mankato, Minn.: Creative Education, 1986.

Rubin, Bob. *All-Stars of the NFL*. New York: Random, 1976.

Sullivan, George. *All About Football*. New York: Putnam, 1990.

How to write to Barry Sanders:

Barry Sanders
c/o Detroit Lions
1200 Featherstone Rd.
Pontiac, Michigan 48342

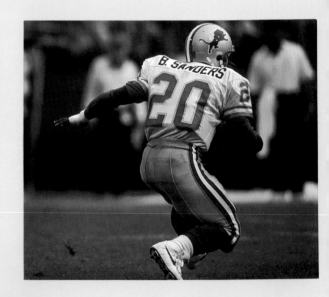

INDEX